D1480931

"**I** live by my wits. I have to be sharp
and clever, lest I go hungry."
—CHARLOTTE

"**I** am naturally a heavy eater and I get untold
satisfaction from the pleasures of the feast."
—TEMPLETON

Wilbur jumped to his feet. "Salu-*what*?" he cried.

"Salutations!" repeated the voice. "Salutations are greetings. When I say 'salutations,' it's just my fancy way of saying hello or good morning. Here I am. Look, I'm waving!"

SALUTATIONS!

WIT AND WISDOM

FROM

Charlotte's Web

BY **E.B. WHITE**

PICTURES BY **GARTH WILLIAMS**

"We take to the breeze, we go as we please."
—CHARLOTTE'S CHILDREN

Fern looked at her father. Then she lifted the lid of the carton. There, inside, looking up at her, was the newborn pig. It was a white one. The morning light shone through its ears, turning them pink.

Fern couldn't take her eyes off the tiny pig. "Oh," she whispered. "Oh, *look* at him! He's absolutely perfect."

In early summer there are plenty of things for a child to eat and drink and suck and chew. Dandelion stems are full of milk, clover heads are loaded with nectar, the Frigidaire is full of ice-cold drinks. Everywhere you look is life; even the little ball of spit on the weed stalk, if you poke it apart, has a green worm inside it.

"Go down through the garden, dig up the radishes! Root up everything! Eat grass! Look for corn! Look for oats! Run all over! Skip and dance, jump and prance! Go down through the orchard and stroll in the woods! The world is a wonderful place when you're young."

—THE GOOSE

Wilbur heard the words of praise. He felt the warm milk inside his stomach. He felt the pleasant rubbing of the stick along his itchy back. He felt peaceful and happy and sleepy. This had been a tiring afternoon. It was still only about four o'clock but Wilbur was ready for bed.

"I'm really too young to go out into the world alone," he thought as he lay down.

"Children pay better attention than grownups."
—Dr. Dorian

Wilbur grunted. He gulped and sucked, and sucked and gulped, making swishing and swooshing noises, anxious to get everything at once. It was a delicious meal—skim milk, wheat middlings, leftover pancakes, half a doughnut, the rind of a summer squash, two pieces of stale toast, a third of a ginger snap, a fish tail, one orange peel, several noodles from a noodle soup, the scum off a cup of cocoa, an ancient jelly roll, a strip of paper from the lining of the garbage pail, and a spoonful of raspberry jello.

"A rat is a rat."

"A rotten egg is a regular stinkbomb."

"Never hurry and never worry!"

"We must advertise Wilbur's noble qualities,
not his tastiness."

—CHARLOTTE

"I've thought all along that that pig of ours was an extra good one. He's a solid pig. He's long, and he's smooth," said Zuckerman.

"That's right," agreed Lurvy. "He's as smooth as they come. He's some pig."

The maples and birches turned bright colors and the wind shook them and they dropped their leaves one by one to the ground. Under the wild apple trees in the pasture, the red little apples lay thick on the ground, and the sheep gnawed them and the geese gnawed them and foxes came in the night and sniffed them.

"The quickest way to spoil a friendship is to wake somebody up in the morning before he is ready."

—THE OLDEST SHEEP

In the daytime, Wilbur usually felt happy and confident. No pig ever had truer friends, and he realized that friendship is one of the most satisfying things in the world.

"My best friends are in the barn cellar."

—Fern

"I prefer to spend my time eating, gnawing, spying, and hiding."

"A rat never knows when something is going to come in handy. I never throw anything away."

"I am glutton but not a merrymaker."
— TEMPLETON

"Perhaps if people talked less, animals
would talk more."

—Dr. Dorian

"If I can fool a bug, I can surely fool a man.
People are not as smart as bugs."

—Charlotte

"People believe almost anything they see in print."
—CHARLOTTE

"With men it's rush, rush, rush every minute."
—CHARLOTTE

Wilbur blushed. "But I'm *not* terrific, Charlotte. I'm just about average for a pig."

"You're terrific as far as *I'm* concerned," replied Charlotte sweetly, "and that's what counts. You're my best friend and *I* think you're sensational. Now stop arguing and go get some sleep!"

"An hour of freedom is worth a barrel of slops."

—THE GOOSE

Wilbur didn't know what to do or which way to run. It seemed as though everybody was after him. "If this is what it's like to be free," he thought, "I believe I'd rather be penned up in my own yard."

"I think you're beautiful," said Wilbur.

"Well, I *am* pretty," replied Charlotte. "There's no denying that."

Wilbur ate his breakfast slowly. He tried to look radiant without getting food in his ears.

Mrs. Zuckerman wasted no time. She climbed in with Wilbur and went to work. Dripping her paddle in the buttermilk, she rubbed him all over. When Mrs. Zuckerman got through and rubbed him dry, he was the cleanest, prettiest pig you ever saw.

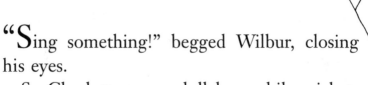

"Sing something!" begged Wilbur, closing his eyes.

So Charlotte sang a lullabye, while crickets chirped in the grass and the barn grew dark. This was the song she sang.

"*Sleep, sleep, my love, my only,*
Deep, deep, in the dung and the dark;
Be not afraid and be not lonely!
This is the hour when frogs and thrushes
Praise the world from the woods and the rushes.
Rest from care, my one and only,
Deep in the dung and the dark!"

After Christmas the thermometer dropped to ten below zero. Cold settled on the world. The pasture was bleak and frozen. The cows stayed in the barn all the time now. The sheep stayed near the barn, too, for protection. When they were thirsty they ate snow. The geese hung around the barnyard the way boys hang around a drug store, and Mr. Zuckerman fed them corn and turnips to keep them cheerful.

Wilbur stood in the sun feeling lonely and bored. He didn't feel like going to sleep, he didn't feel like digging, he was tired of standing still, tired of lying down.

"When I'm out here," he said, "there's no place to go but in. When I'm indoors, there's no place to go but out in the yard."

—Wilbur

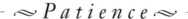

"After four weeks of unremitting effort
and patience on the part of our friend the
goose, she now has something to show
for it. The goslings have arrived."

—CHARLOTTE

Charlotte was naturally patient. She knew from experience that if she waited long enough, a fly would come to her web.

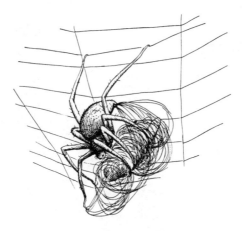

"What do you mean, *less* than nothing? I don't think there is any such thing as less than nothing. Nothing is absolutely the limit of nothingness. It's the lowest you can go. It's the end of the line. How can something be less than nothing? If there were something that was less than nothing, then nothing would not be nothing, it would be something—even though it's just a very little bit of something. But if nothing is *nothing*, then nothing has nothing that is less than *it* is."

—WILBUR

"Take a deep breath! Now climb to the highest place you can get to. Now make an attachment with your spinnerets, hurl yourself into space, and let out a dragline as you go down!"

—CHARLOTTE

"What does sedentary mean?" asked Wilbur.

"Means I sit still a good part of the time and don't go wandering all over creation. I stay put and wait for what comes. Gives me a chance to think."

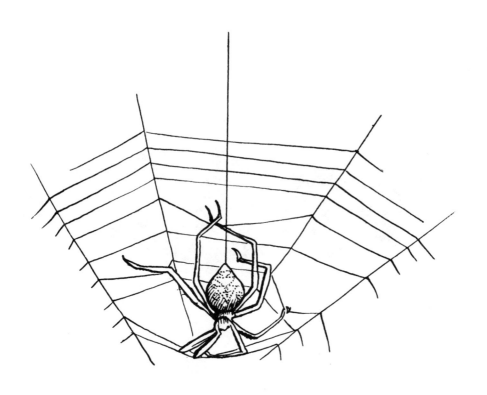

"Humble?" said Charlotte. "'Humble' has two meanings. It means 'not proud' and it means 'near the ground.' That's Wilbur all over. He's not proud and he's near the ground."

"I don't know what a magnum opus is," said Wilbur.

"That's Latin," explained Charlotte. "It means 'great work'. This egg sac is my great work—the finest thing I have ever made."

"You have been my friend," replied Charlotte. "That in itself is a tremendous thing. I wove my webs for you because I liked you. After all, what's a life anyway? We're born, we live a little while, we die. A spider's life can't help being something of a mess, with all this trapping and eating flies. By helping you, perhaps I was trying to lift up my life a trifle. Heaven knows anyone's life can stand a little of that."

~ *Spring* ~

The snows melted and ran away. The streams and ditches bubbled and chattered with rushing water. A sparrow with a streaky breast arrived and sang. The light strengthened, the mornings came sooner. Almost every morning there was another new lamb in the sheepfold. The goose was sitting on nine eggs. The sky seemed wider and a warm wind blew.

Wilbur's heart brimmed with happiness. "Joy! Aranea! Nellie!" he began. "Welcome to the barn cellar. You have chosen a hallowed doorway from which to string your webs. I think it is only fair to tell you that I was devoted to your mother. I owe my very life to her. She was brilliant, beautiful, and loyal to the end. I shall always treasure her memory. To you, her daughters, I pledge my friendship, forever and ever."

Wilbur never forgot Charlotte. Although he loved her children and grandchildren dearly, none of the new spiders ever quite took her place in his heart. She was in a class by herself. It is not often that someone comes along who is a true friend and a good writer. Charlotte was both.

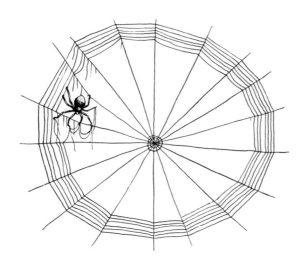